# The

# Wealth Factor

# Workbook

## By
## Amanda Rose

Amanda Rose

## DAY 1: MINDSET

What's the Basics of the Law of Attraction?

_____

_____

_____


When I'm thinking, ____ and _____ are irrelevant to the Universe. Because of that, I need to focus on thinking only about _____.


Money Mindset starts with my beliefs. The creation process is, _____ create our _____, our _____ create our _____, our _____ dictate our _____, and our _____ create our _____.


Where my Beliefs Come From (Childhood)
As a child, how do I remember money being discussed?

_____

_____

_____

_____


Did we have a lot of money or not very much?

_____

_____

_____

_____

Were your needs always met?

_____
_____
_____
_____
_____

Was there 1 or more significant event you remember about money? How did it make you feel?

_____
_____
_____
_____
_____
_____
_____

What repeated sayings do you remember hearing about money?

_____
_____
_____
_____
_____
_____
_____
_____

Based on these answers, what do you think you picked up as your beliefs about money?

_____
_____
_____
_____
_____
_____
_____
_____
_____
_____

Do you notice some habits your parents/guardians had about money that you are living out in your own life?

_____
_____
_____
_____
_____
_____
_____
_____
_____
_____
_____
_____
_____
_____

Where my Beliefs Come From (Adolescence-Age 25)
In your adolescence, teens, and early adulthood, what were your experiences around money and work?

_____

_____

_____

_____

_____

_____

_____

_____

_____

_____

_____

_____

In your first dating and romantic experiences, were there any negative situations around money (feeling expected to pay, feeling unworthy because you were unable to afford to take a person out, etc.)?

_____

_____

_____

_____

_____

_____

_____

Did you find yourself rebelling against your parent's way of handling money?

_____

_____

_____

_____

_____

_____

_____

_____

_____

What specific money situations come to mind? How do they make you feel?

_____

_____

_____

_____

_____

_____

_____

_____

_____

_____

_____

_____

_____

_____

_____

# What Beliefs do you Feel you Picked up During Your First 25 years of Your Life?

_____

_____

_____

_____

_____

_____

_____

_____

_____

_____

_____

_____

_____

_____

_____

_____

_____

_____

_____

_____

_____

Review your responses, release the beliefs that don't support who you want to become, and then re-write your beliefs to support the success you want:

Old Belief: _____

New Belief: _____


Old Belief: _____

New Belief: _____


Old Belief: _____

New Belief: _____


Old Belief: _____

New Belief: _____


Old Belief: _____

New Belief: _____


Old Belief: _____

New Belief: _____


Old Belief: _____

New Belief: _____


Old Belief: _____

New Belief: _____


Old Belief: _____

New Belief: _____

What Money is: _____
_____
_____

What Money is NOT: _____
_____
_____

My Letter to Money...

Dear Money,
_____
_____
_____
_____
_____
_____
_____
_____
_____
_____
_____
_____
_____
_____
_____

Sincerely,
_____

## What I love About Money Is...

_____

_____

_____

_____

_____

_____

_____

_____

_____

_____

_____

## I Love Rich People!

I looked up _____ and when I read about
their story I learned that _____

_____

_____

_____

_____

_____

_____

_____

_____

I, _____, commit to be a No Matter
What Person!

# Day 1: Mindset | Video Notes

_____
_____
_____
_____
_____
_____
_____
_____
_____
_____
_____
_____
_____
_____
_____
_____
_____
_____
_____
_____
_____
_____
_____
_____
_____

# Day 2: Wealth Building

Money Management

| Income Source | $ Amount | Expense Source | $ Amount |
|---|---|---|---|
|  |  |  |  |
|  |  |  |  |
|  |  |  |  |
|  |  |  |  |
|  |  |  |  |
|  |  |  |  |
|  |  |  |  |
|  |  |  |  |
|  |  |  |  |
|  |  |  |  |
|  |  |  |  |
|  |  |  |  |
|  |  |  |  |
| TOTAL: | $ | TOTAL: | $ |

Income Total _____ - Expenses Total _____

= _____ remaining.

## Shaving Down Expenses

Where can I shave down my expenses?

_____

_____

_____

_____

_____

_____

_____

_____

How much will this save me annually? _____

_____

_____

_____

_____

_____

_____

The 4 Accounts I need to Set up to manage my money are:

1.

2.

3.

4.

Income Types:

Working Income is _____
_____
_____
_____
_____

Residual Income is _____
_____
_____
_____

Passive Income is _____
_____
_____
_____

Dividend Payouts are _____
_____
_____
_____

Royalties are _____
_____
_____
_____
_____

_____
_____
_____
_____
_____
_____
_____
_____
_____
_____
_____
_____
_____
_____
_____
_____
_____
_____
_____
_____
_____
_____
_____
_____
_____
_____
_____
_____

# Day 2: Wealth Builder | General Notes

# DAY 3: ACTION

Inner Work Game Plan

The Morning Routine I'm Committing to Every Day is:

_____

_____

_____

_____

_____

_____

The Nighttime Routine I'm Committing to Every Day is:

_____

_____

_____

_____

_____

_____

_____

My emotions are my barometer, so while moving ahead I will be leaning into _____.

Everything is cyclical, I must remember the economy will always _____.

I need to act in spite of _____.

## Outer Work Game Plan Checklist:

I have done the 'Know Where you Stand' exercise from day 2, so I understand my total income is _____ and my total expenses are _____, giving me _____ left over.

☐

 *Check This Box once You've Completed This

I have opened up my four accounts, _____, _____, _____, and _____.

☐

*Check This Box once You've Completed This

The 3 ways I've picked to start shaving down my expenses are:

1.

2.

3.

☐

*Check This Box once You've Completed This

The first investing option I am going to learn about and will be taking action on is, _____.

☐

*Check This Box once You've Completed This

The financial planner I am going to see is _____ And my first appointment with them is, _____

☐

*Check This Box once You've Completed This

## Skills

Marketing

Marketing is _____
_____
_____

My Niche is _____
_____
_____
_____
_____

My Message is _____
_____
_____
_____
_____

My Brand is _____
_____
_____
_____
_____
_____
_____

## SALES

What are 'Sales'? _____
_____
_____
_____
_____

What Problem does my Product/Service Solve? _____
_____
_____
_____
_____

I sell by _____

Follow ups are important because _____
_____
_____
_____

I Can Leverage My Business By _____
_____
_____
_____
_____
_____
_____
_____

## Commit

The final step is to commit. Commit to making the changes. Commit to a mindset practice. Commit to learning how to make your money make you MORE money. Commit to taking action, every single day, to shift your financial reality.

Making money isn't about the money, it's about giving yourself freedom and unlimited choices. Wealth is simply about you tapping into the abundance of life so that you can do, be, and have whatever you want and need that will allow you to live a fulfilled life.

I, _____, commit to working on my money mindset, learning about how to turn money into more money, and taking action. I commit to living a truly abundant life, in every sense of the word!

# NOTES

_____
_____
_____
_____
_____
_____
_____
_____
_____
_____
_____
_____
_____
_____
_____
_____
_____
_____
_____
_____
_____

_____

_____

_____

_____

_____

_____

_____

_____

_____

_____

_____

_____

_____

_____

_____

_____

_____

_____

_____

_____

_____

# This Workbook Is the Companion Guide for The Wealth Factor Course

## The Wealth Factor Intensive

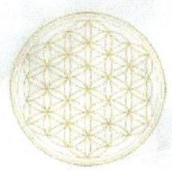

In this 3-Day Intensive you'll get the financial education that you never got in school! Learning the way that the rich and successful think, you'll get the mindset strategies and money management advise to turn your financial reality around!

**Learn More:** https://amanda-rose.mykajabi.com/courses

# A Few of Amanda's Other Courses...

Master your mindset and you master your life! The key to success, wealth, happiness, health, and all of the good things you WANT in your life are unlocked through your mindset!

In this special 90-Minute Mastermind I will teach you...

🌙 How your thoughts have been dictating your results

🌙 Why mastering your mindset is the key to your success

🌙 Why you are where you are based on your past conditioning

🌙 How to reprogram your mind to support you in creating the life you've always wanted

🌙 How to retrain your mind to support you instead of hinder you

🌙 How you can have MORE fun and make MORE money while you Work LESS

🌙 And much more...

A 90-Minute session with me would normally cost $375, but for this Mindset Mastery 90-Minute Mastermind you're going to get in for JUST $11!!!

**Contact Amanda to Gain Access**
Amanda@AmandaRoseFitness.com

This is a 5-Day workshop that will take you through everything from how to choose your topic, structure your course, create content, and how to market and sell it!

In 5-Days You'll have ALL of the skills you need to create and launch your course!

You're going to get...

✨The #1 Insider Secret to Creating a Course that Sells VS one That Flops

✨Step-By-Step walk-through on creating your course from concept to launch

✨Daily Video Training

✨Daily Written Training

✨1:1 Messenger and Voice Message Access to Amanda for Individual Help

✨Launch Strategies

✨Course Creation Workbook PDF

Are you ready to create your course, help others learn, and expand your biz?! Let's do this!

**This 5-Day workshop is just $222. Register Here:**
https://amanda-rose.mykajabi.com/offers/RLeeQAhF

In the Money Mastery 90-Minute Mindset Gurus, Xerces A Lewis Your Intuitive Soul Doctor, and Amanda Rose Mindset Coach & Author of the Manifesting Series will help you...

💰 To heal your relationship with money so that you naturally begin to attract it

💰 To understand the true meaning of wealth and abundance so that you aren't subconsciously repelling it

💰 Learn what they NEVER taught you in school about wealth creation

💰 Understand how the rich think differently from the poor & the middle class

💰 To get into the energetic flow of money so that you become a money magnet!

95% of wealthy people started with nothing. That means YOU can too!

We're going to show you the path, the only question is... are you ready to walk it?

A 90-Minute session with Myself and Xerces would normally cost $565, but for this Mindset Mastery 90-Minute Mastermind you're going to get in for JUST $88!

**Contact Amanda to Gain Access**
Amanda@AmandaRoseFitness.com

This course is going to cover everything from the writing process, to editing, formatting, and publishing, and how to successfully market your book. what works and how to do it properly, and what to avoid. It's compiling over a year's worth of research, so you don't have to spend endless hours trying to figure out what to do to get your book recognized, in the press, into bookstores, libraries, and land book signings.

If you're ready to finally write your book, get it out in the world, and generate an incredible income through book royalties, then it's time to sign up for this 3-week online workshop!

**Learn More:**
https://amanda-rose.mykajabi.com/offers/7bUzKNX2/checkout

## About the Author

Amanda Rose is an avid reader and storyteller. Working in a variety of mediums and genres, communicating new ways of thinking is her passion.

Amanda works as an online Health and Fitness coach, Mindset & Business Coach, Actor, Model, Motivational Speaker, Online Course Creator and Writer.

Residing in Kingston, Ontario, with her husband and 3 cats, Amanda is currently working on her next novel. Get in touch with Amanda by visiting her website:

HTTPS://Amanda-rose.mykajabi.com

# Manifesting Your Best Life

## Manifesting Your Best Life Book Description:

Stop dreaming about a better life and start living it!

Manifesting You Best Life is going to show you that "Living Your Best Life" isn't just some cute meme on social media – it can be your way of life! The 21 nugget-of-wisdom chapters in this self-help book are for people who want to start living their best life, but don't know where to begin. It will give you the skills to take you from dreaming about your best life, to making it your reality!

You will learn:
•How to Identify what living your best life really means to you.
•The steps needed to stop wishing and start living your best life.
•How to use the Law of Attraction to support your efforts.
•Successful habits that will change your life.
•And how to create the life you've always wanted... And start living it NOW!

By the end of Manifesting Your Best Life, you will have a clear picture of what your dream life looks like, how to get there, and the tools and skills to make it into your reality!

Are you ready to begin?

## ALSO AVAILABLE ON AUDIBLE

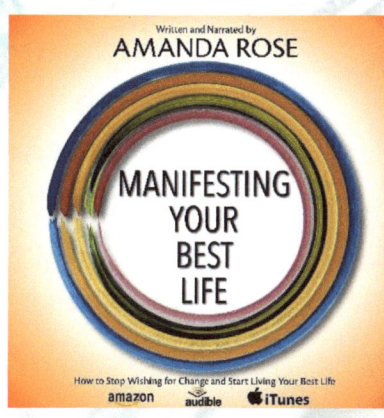

# The Manifesting 30-Day Guided Journal

*From the author of Manifesting on Purpose comes The Manifesting 30-Day Guided Journal!*

## This Law of Attraction Based Journal will take your Manifesting Practice to The Next Level!

The Manifesting 30-Day Guided Journal will walk you through 30 days of curated activities that will get you into the energetic flow of manifestation. Through goal-setting, mindfulness, clarity, and actionable steps, you will learn how to create the life of happiness and freedom that you've always desired.

## The Orgasmic Cookbook

### The Orgasmic Cookbook Book Description:

*Nutrition Meets Flavor.*

Just because it's healthy doesn't mean it should be boring. In *The Orgasmic Cookbook* Amanda teaches her best tips and tricks to make healthy food pop with flavor! Having lost over 100 pounds Amanda knows the importance of eating healthy. As a food lover she's made it her mission to create healthy recipes packed with rich taste!

Get ready for mouth-watering recipes that will give you a whole new appreciation for food!

## Manifesting on Purpose

## Manifesting on Purpose Book Description:

It's time to take manifesting off auto-pilot, get behind the wheel, and start steering your life in the direction you want it to go!

Manifesting on Purpose clarifies why we manifest what we do, why we experience the same things over and over again, until we step in and weed out our own mental gardens.

Ever wonder how is it that 2 people can start off with the same opportunity, and one will become a massive success, while the other barely scrapes by? What's the defining factor?

What do successful people know that we're missing? We've been taught that the harder we work the more money, happiness, and success we'll have in life; but if this was the case successful people would constantly we run ragged, and be bleary eyed from lack of sleep, instead of enjoying lots of free time pursuing their heart's desires. So, what are we missing?

The Law of Attraction is always working, even when we're not focused on it. The Law of Attraction states that, "Like Attracts Like," we are all energy, so our thoughts get reflected back to us. Your thoughts create your physical reality. The problem? We're always thinking! Our thoughts, ungoverned, bounce around from idea to idea, and all too often, focus on the immediate problems in our lives, creating a feedback loop. Since we attract back what we think about, if we're focused on our problems, what's going to show up? More problems!

Your mind is your most valuable asset. Your thoughts literally create your reality. Your current situation is a reflection of your previous thoughts. Most people, however, do not consciously decide what they want, their subconscious belief systems run everything on auto-pilot; making most people feel as if they are victims of their circumstances. YOU ARE NOT A VICTIM OF CIRCUMSTANCE!

You are in the driver's seat, you simply have to take control of the wheel! Take manifesting off auto-pilot and create the life you want! "But I think positive thoughts," you say. Your conscious thoughts will always be secondary to your subconscious thoughts in the way of manifestation. Until you change your core beliefs to line up with who you wish to become, and what you wish to do, you cannot break the old cycles.

Are you ready to take control? Have abundance in money, love, health, freedom, experiences, and all other areas of your life? Then let's get started!

# Manifesting Money: How to Master and Apply Abundance Mindset in Your Life

**Manifesting Money Book description: Master Your Mindset and You Master Your Life!**

Why does 99% of the population struggle financially? Is it a lack of opportunity? An issue with education? Not having the right skills? Poor investment choices? Bad timing? Low work performance?

The startling answer is: none of the above!

Wealth creation is a mindset.

It's not what rich people *do*, but how they *think* that sets them apart. *Manifesting Money* is going to teach you how to:

•Discover and Get Rid of Money Blocks

•Kick Fear and Doubt to the Curb

•Create New Supportive Money Beliefs

•Develop Wealth Consciousness

•Build Multiple Sources of Income

•Work Smarter Not Harder

•Manage Money

•Implement the Successful Habits Rich People Use

•Have the Wealth You've Always Wanted

It's time to start *Manifesting Money*!

# Get Published Workbook: Write | Publish | Market

### Get Published Workbook Book Description:

Most people have thought about publishing a book, but the majority will never even begin writing one. Why? The process can seem daunting. Conceptualizing, writing, editing, formatting, copywriting, publishing, and finally marketing; it can seem like an overwhelming amount of work when you aren't sure what each step entails.

In this workbook, you're going to learn all of my best practices so you can go from concept to published in 2-6 months pending on the length and style of your book, with full knowledge of what to expect, and what to do, so nothing will stand in your way of becoming a successful author!

Self-publishing is an incredible avenue to get your work to your readers fast, with widespread distribution, that allows you to take the lion's share of the profits for the book you put all the work into creating!

With self-publishing, you're in control, but that also means you are in charge of your own marketing campaign. Don't let that scare you away! With social media and online sales booming, you can reach your ideal reader audience easier, and at much less cost, than with traditional marketing. You just need to learn how!

**Through this book, you're going to learn...**
• How to brainstorm and develop a concept
• How to effectively begin writing your book
• How to create disciplined habits to finish your book
• How to edit, format, and polish your book so it's ready for publication
• Why reviews are the life-blood of self-publishing, and how to get them
• How to write an effective book description
• How to write a gripping back cover
• Why your book cover is your most important investment
• How the self-publishing process works
• Best practices for ultimate exposure
• How to use inexpensive pay-per-click campaigns to drive traffic
• Social Media Marketing
• Free marketing practices
• Inexpensive marketing options
• Importance of an author web site to boost SEO
...And much more!

## Fire Fury Freedom

"A veritable saga of a dystopian novel by an author with a genuine flair for detailed originality, and narrative driven storytelling, "Fire Fury Freedom" by Amanda Rose is an extraordinary and truly memorable read from cover to cover." -*Midwest Book Review*

**Prequel to the Fire Fury Frontier Series**

### Fire Fury Freedom Book Description:

A dying planet on the verge of collapse.... tormented pasts that haunt the present... an ancient hidden magick...

The C.D.F.P. mega-corporation rules all, with unchecked power, and dark secrets...

The planet is dying, and they are the last hope to save it... Mack, an ex-soldier of the C.D.F.P. military division, and his mercenaries, standalone against the C.D.F.P. (AKA the Company), in the fight for humanities survival. Left unchallenged, the company has ruled over the East Green Continent with an iron fist for decades. The pollution they've caused has devastated the planet, destroying the ozone, and killing off plant and animal life.

Outside of domed cities the air is thin, and the sun scorches all; it's a veritable wasteland. In the past two decades the planet has reached entirely new levels of decay. Extreme weather patterns, and massive quakes, ravage the land.

Time is running out...

Mack and his mercenary troupe set out on a quest to stop the C.D.F.P. once and for all, and the planet will test them to their limits... But are they ready for the horrors they'll uncover? Can they alone stand up against the all-powerful C.D.F.P.?

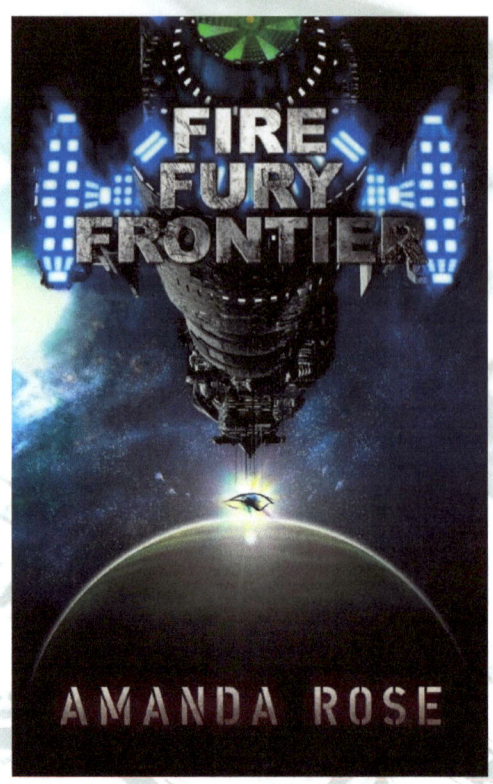

## Fire Fury Frontier

### Fire Fury Frontier Book Description:

One ship, one last chance to survive...

Humanity's home world has been destroyed from extensive global warming. For over two hundred years the last remaining humans have lived in space aboard a single massive ship, the Saisei. After generations in space, living aboard a ship is all anyone has ever known.

But space is an inhospitable home.

The ship is old and damaged, rations are low, and a planet fit for colonization has never been found.

In the vast expanse of space, as the Saisei makes way to resupply their ship, they stumble upon a discovery that will change the course of human history forever.

## ALSO AVAILABLE ON AUDIBLE

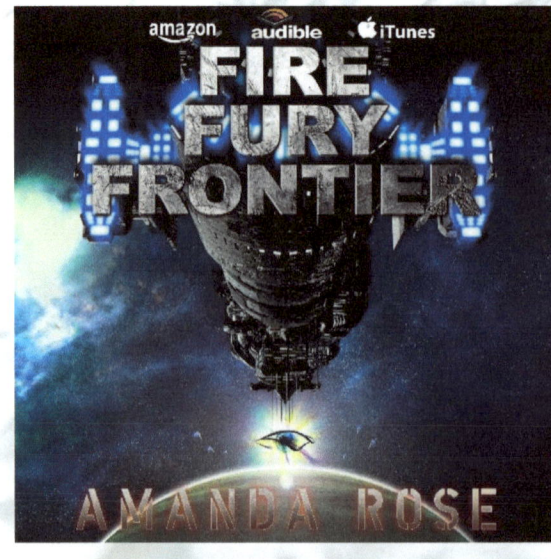

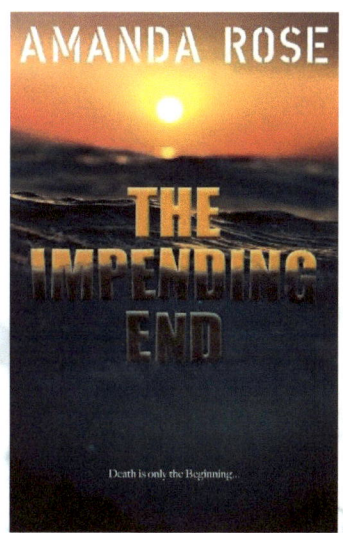

# The Impending End

### The Impending End Book Description:

It's 2005. Ayla Jefferson is 17, incredibly intelligent, sensitive, imaginative, and thoughtful. She's also contemplating suicide...

After a life long battle with mental illness plaguing her every move, Ayla is ready for death. Eerily calm, she says her goodbyes, and sets out to commit her final act.

But despite her stubborn conviction, life isn't as easy to let go of as she expected. Her hyper-imagination blurs reality and she finds herself getting lost in gripping memories. Mentally disengaged, Ayla's experiences are surreal, and discerning fact from fiction becomes harder and harder.

As the life she's so eager to leave behind begs to hold on, will she be able to leave it all behind?

## A Strange Dream: Anthology of Short Stories and Poetry

## A Strange Dream Book Description:

Death, Depression, Insomnia, Prostitution, Eating Disorders, Abortion, Convicts, Insanity, and Marital issues... This anthology of short stories and poetry explores the dark reaches of the mind and mental health issues.

The 9 short stories, including award winning EGGS and OUTSIDER, as well as runner up in the Canadian Writer's Guild Short Prose competition, DROWNING IN SILENCE, and 9 poems, take us on a journey from the surreal to the mundane. From day-to-day life to fantasy, the characters and situations explore many walks of life.

www.ingramcontent.com/pod-product-compliance
Lightning Source LLC
Chambersburg PA
CBHW041816200526
45172CB00026B/806